THE REAL LAW
What they don't want you to know

BY
Zeth Krause

I have done all the work for you so it isn't hard to find all these documents
that they hide deep in the books.
Most law enforcement don't even know this stuff.

Rights Act from the U.S.C

Legal Notice And Demand

Affidavit Of Truth

Color Of Law

Flex your rights on last page

Title 18, U.S.C., Section 249
Matthew Shepard and James Byrd, Jr., Hate Crimes Prevention Act

This statute makes it unlawful to willfully cause bodily injury—or attempting to do so with fire, firearm, or other dangerous weapon—when 1) the crime was committed because of the actual or perceived race, color, religion, national origin of any person, or 2) the crime was committed because of the actual or perceived religion, national origin, gender, sexual orientation, gender identity, or disability of any person and the crime affected interstate or foreign commerce or occurred within federal special maritime and territorial jurisdiction.

The law also provides funding and technical assistance to state, local, and tribal jurisdictions to help them to more effectively investigate, prosecute, and prevent hate crimes.

The law provides for a maximum 10-year prison term, unless death (or attempts to kill) results from the offense, or unless the offense includes kidnapping or attempted kidnapping, or aggravated sexual abuse or attempted aggravated sexual abuse. For offenses not resulting in death, there is a seven-year statute of limitations. For offenses resulting in death, there is no statute of limitations.

Title 18, U.S.C., Section 241
Conspiracy Against Rights

This statute makes it unlawful for two or more persons to conspire to injure, oppress, threaten, or intimidate any person of any state, territory or district in the free exercise or enjoyment of any right or privilege secured to him/her by the Constitution or the laws of the United States, (or because of his/her having exercised the same).

It further makes it unlawful for two or more persons to go in disguise on the highway or on the premises of another with the intent to prevent or hinder his/her free exercise or enjoyment of any rights so secured.

Punishment varies from a fine or imprisonment of up to ten years, or both; and if death results, or if such acts include kidnapping or an attempt to kidnap, aggravated sexual abuse or an attempt to commit aggravated sexual abuse, or an attempt to kill, shall be fined under this title or imprisoned for any term of years, or for life, or may be sentenced to death.

Title 18, U.S.C., Section 242
Deprivation of Rights Under Color of Law

This statute makes it a crime for any person acting under color of law, statute, ordinance, regulation, or custom to willfully deprive or cause to be deprived from any person those rights, privileges, or immunities secured or protected by the Constitution and laws of the U.S.

This law further prohibits a person acting under color of law, statute, ordinance, regulation or custom to willfully subject or cause to be subjected any person to different punishments, pains, or penalties, than those prescribed for punishment of citizens on account of such person being an alien or by reason of his/her color or race.

Acts under "color of any law" include acts not only done by federal, state, or local officials within the bounds or limits of their lawful authority, but also acts done without and beyond the bounds of their lawful authority; provided that, in order for unlawful acts of any official to be done under "color of any law," the unlawful acts must be done while such official is purporting or pretending to act in the performance of his/her official duties. This definition includes, in addition to law enforcement officials, individuals such as Mayors, Council persons, Judges, Nursing Home Proprietors, Security Guards, etc., persons who are bound by laws, statutes ordinances, or customs.

Punishment varies from a fine or imprisonment of up to one year, or both, and if bodily injury results or if such acts include the use, attempted use, or threatened use of a dangerous weapon, explosives, or fire shall be fined or imprisoned up to ten years or both, and if death results, or if such acts include kidnapping or an attempt to kidnap, aggravated sexual abuse or an attempt to commit aggravated sexual abuse, or an attempt to kill, shall be fined under this title, or imprisoned for any term of years or for life, or both, or may be sentenced to death.

Title 18, U.S.C., Section 245
Federally Protected Activities

1) This statute prohibits willful injury, intimidation, or interference, or attempt to do so, by force or threat of force of any person or class of persons because of their activity as:

a) A voter, or person qualifying to vote...;
b) a participant in any benefit, service, privilege, program, facility, or activity provided or administered by the United States;
c) an applicant for federal employment or an employee by the federal government;

d) a juror or prospective juror in federal court; and
e) a participant in any program or activity receiving Federal financial assistance.
2) Prohibits willful injury, intimidation, or interference or attempt to do so, by force or threat of force of any person because of race, color, religion, or national origin and because of his/her activity as:
a) A student or applicant for admission to any public school or public college;
b) a participant in any benefit, service, privilege, program, facility, or activity provided or administered by a state or local government;
c) an applicant for private or state employment, private or state employee; a member or applicant for membership in any labor organization or hiring hall; or an applicant for employment through any employment agency, labor organization or hiring hall;
d) a juror or prospective juror in state court;
e) a traveler or user of any facility of interstate commerce or common carrier; or
f) a patron of any public accommodation, including hotels, motels, restaurants, lunchrooms, bars, gas stations, theaters...or any other establishment which serves the public and which is principally engaged in selling food or beverages for consumption on the premises.
3) Prohibits interference by force or threat of force against any person because he/she is or has been, or in order to intimidate such person or any other person or class of persons from participating or affording others the opportunity or protection to so participate, or lawfully aiding or encouraging other persons to participate in any of the benefits or activities listed in items (1) and (2), above without discrimination as to race, color, religion, or national origin.
Punishment varies from a fine or imprisonment of up to one year, or both, and if bodily injury results or if such acts include the use, attempted use, or threatened use of a dangerous weapon, explosives, or fire shall be fined or imprisoned up to ten years or both, and if death results or if such acts include kidnapping or an attempt to kidnap, aggravated sexual abuse or an attempt to commit aggravated sexual abuse, or an attempt to kill, shall be subject to imprisonment for any term of years or for life or may be sentenced to death.

Title 18, U.S.C., Section 247
Church Arson Prevention Act of 1996

Prohibits (1) intentional defacement, damage, or destruction of any religious real property, because of the religious, racial, or ethnic characteristics of that property, or (2) intentional obstruction by force or threat of force, or attempts to obstruct any person in the enjoyment of that person's free exercise of religious beliefs. If the intent of the crime is motivated for reasons of religious animosity, it must be proven that the religious real property has a sufficient connection with interstate or foreign commerce. However, if the intent of the crime is racially motivated, there is no

requirement to satisfy the interstate or foreign commerce clause.
Punishment varies from one year imprisonment and a fine or both, and if bodily injury results to any person, including any public safety officer performing duties as a direct or proximate result of conduct prohibited by this section, and the violation is by means of fire or an explosive, a fine under this title or imprisonment of not more than forty years or both; or if such acts include the use, attempted use, or threatened use of a dangerous weapon, explosives, or fire shall be fined in accordance with this title and imprisonment for up to twenty years, or both, and if death results or if such acts include kidnapping or an attempt to kidnap, aggravated sexual abuse or an attempt to commit aggravated sexual abuse, or an attempt to kill, shall be fined in accordance with this title and imprisoned for any term of years or for life, or both, or may be sentenced to death.

Title 18, U.S.C., Section 248
Freedom of Access to Clinic Entrances (FACE) Act

This statute prohibits (1) the use of force or threat of force or physical obstruction, to intentionally injure, intimidate or interfere with or attempt to injure, intimidate or interfere with any person or any class of persons from obtaining or providing reproductive health services; (2) the use of force or threat of force or physical obstruction to intentionally injure, intimidate, or interfere with or attempt to injure, intimidate, or interfere with any person lawfully exercising or seeking to exercise the First Amendment right of religious freedom at a place of religious worship; or (3) intentionally damages or destroys the property of a facility, or attempts to do so, because such facility provides reproductive health services or intentionally damages or destroys the property of a place of religious worship. This statute does not apply to speech or expressive conduct protected by the First Amendment. Non obstructive demonstrations are legal.

Punishment varies from a fine or imprisonment for an offense involving exclusively a nonviolent physical obstruction, the fine shall be not more than $10,000 and the length of imprisonment shall be up to six months, or both, for the first offense: and the fine shall, notwithstanding section 3571, be up to $25,000 and the length of imprisonment shall be not more than 18 months, or both, for a subsequent offense; and if bodily injury results, the length of imprisonment shall be up to ten years, and if death results, it shall be for any term of years or for life.

Title 18, U.S.C., Section 844(h)
Federal Explosives Control Statute

Whoever (1) uses fire or an explosive to commit any felony which may be prosecuted in a court of the United States, or (2) carries an explosive during the commission of any felony which may be prosecuted in a court of the United States, including a felony which provides for an enhanced punishment if committed by the use of a deadly or dangerous weapon or device shall, in addition to the punishment provided for such felony, be sentenced to imprisonment for five years but not more than 15 years. In the case of a second or subsequent conviction under this subsection, such persons shall be sentenced to imprisonment for ten years but not more than 25 years.

Title 42, U.S.C., Section 3631
Criminal Interference with Right to Fair Housing

This statute makes it unlawful for any individual(s), by the use of force or threatened use of force, to injure, intimidate, or interfere with (or attempt to injure, intimidate, or interfere with), any person's housing rights because of that person's race, color, religion, sex, handicap, familial status or national origin. Among those housing rights enumerated in the statute are:

- The sale, purchase, or renting of a dwelling;
- the occupation of a dwelling;
- the financing of a dwelling;
- contracting or negotiating for any of the rights enumerated above.
- applying for or participating in any service, organization, or facility relating to the sale or rental of dwellings.

This statute also makes it unlawful by the use of force or threatened use of force, to injure, intimidate, or interfere with any person who is assisting an individual or class of persons in the exercise of their housing rights.

Punishment varies from a fine of up to $1,000 or imprisonment of up to one year, or both, and if bodily injury results, shall be fined up to $10,000 or imprisoned up to ten years, or both, and if death results, shall be subject to imprisonment for any term of years or for life.

Title 42, U.S.C., Section 14141
Pattern and Practice

This civil statute was a provision within the Crime Control Act of 1994 and makes it unlawful for any governmental authority, or agent thereof, or any person acting on behalf of a governmental authority, to engage in a pattern or practice of conduct by law enforcement officers or by officials or employees of any governmental agency with responsibility for the administration of juvenile justice or the incarceration of juveniles that deprives persons of rights, privileges, or immunities secured or protected by the Constitution or laws of the United States.

Whenever the Attorney General has reasonable cause to believe that a violation has occurred, the Attorney General, for or in the name of the United States, may in a civil action obtain appropriate equitable and declaratory relief to eliminate the pattern or practice.

Types of misconduct covered include, among other things:
1. Excessive Force
2. Discriminatory Harassment
3. False Arrest
4. Coercive Sexual Conduct
5. Unlawful Stops, Searches, or Arrests

International Registered Private Tracking Number – REGISTERED MAIL# ON B/C BOND

Act of State, Reaffirmation of Character, State of YOUR STATE APOSTILLE No. 12345678

YOUR STATE UCC – Secured Transaction Registry Number – 123456789 -
ADDENDUM

ATTENTION! AND WARNING!

THIS IS A LEGAL NOTICE AND DEMAND

FIAT JUSTITIA, RUAT COELUM

(Let right be done, though the heavens should fall)

NON WAR POWERS through ACT FLAG SECRETARY.

To: All State, Federal and International Public Officials, by and YOUR STATE SECRETARY OF STATE NAME OF SECRETARY.

TAKE NOTICE IGNORANCE OF THE LAW IS NO EXCUSE!

THIS IS A CONTRACT IN ADMIRALTY JURISDICTION

Take a moment to read this before you proceed any further!

I do not wish to speak to you under any circumstances excluding federal judicial review!

THIS TITLE IS FOR YOUR PROTECTION!

(1) I, One First-Middle:[LastName]**,** [Freeman] the undersigned herein requests anything you say to me you present in writing signed under penalty of perjury required by your law as shown on page eight of this instrument infra ¶20. **Notice to Agent is Notice to Principal. Notice to Principal is notice to Agent.** Attachments are included and are part of this contract.

(2) This notice is in nature of a Miranda Warning. Take due heed of contents. If, for *any* reason, you do not understand *any* of these statements or warnings, it is incumbent upon you to summon a superior officer, special prosecutor or federal judge, or other competent legal counsel, to immediately explain to you the significance of this presentment as per your duties and obligations in respect to this private formal notarized "registered" **Statute Staple Securities Instrument.**

PAGE TWO LEGAL NOTICE AND DEMAND

(3) Your failure to timely do so leaves you in the position of accepting full responsibility for *any* and *all* liabilities for monetary damages, as indicated herein, that I incur by any adversely affecting injury(s) *caused* by your overt, or covert actions, or the action(s) of *any* of your fellow (public) officers and agents in this or *any* other relevant matter(s) as described herein. You have Thirty (30) days, from the date this document is received by the Clerk of the Public Record, to respond and rebut the presumptions of this contract by submitting to me signed, certified, authenticated documents of the laws that rebut these presumptions point by point, On and For the Record under penalties of the law including perjury. This document will be on file in the public record and the clerk in charge of the public record is charged to distribute this to any and all responsible parties i.e., officers of the court, and/or law enforcement officers including local, state, federal, International, Multi-jurisdictional, or any and all officers, representatives, contractors, agencies, or any such entity or person, that may bring any type of action, whether civil or criminal or other, against me, and whether in this county, state, region, area, country, corporation, or Federal Zone or in any venue and/or jurisdiction. Your Failure to timely rebut the statements and warnings herein constitute your complete tacit agreement with all statements and warnings contained herein. Your presumptions that I, the undersigned, am a "Corporate Fiction", or "Legal Entity" and under your corporate "UNITED STATES" jurisdiction are now and forever rebutted.

(4) The undersigned tendering this document is a Private People of Posterity; a Sovereign Personam Sojourn; by fact; **not** a 14th amendment citizen or surety within; or subject for; or allegiance to; your corporate UNITED STATES; or to *any* de facto compact (Corporate) commercial states contracting therein; Only to the United States of America, nonetheless carrying with me exclusive original sovereign jurisdiction and venue having one supreme Court and United States Court of International Trade. Now being a matter of public record, rendered by way of "registered mail" to YOUR STATE Secretary of State. Hence recorded pages upon Liber Records and Books from "Register of Deeds Offices" from but not limited too; YOUR COUNTY AND SURROUNDING COUNTIES, further but not limited to; all (YOUR STATE) State Land and or Public Notices in County Paper of Records United States of America **Idem.**

(5) The party now tendering this legally binding "NOTICE and DEMAND" in hand is not a surety; under your jurisdiction, or a subject under your corporate veil "color of law venue", being acknowledged by silence and acquiescence of NAME OF SECRETARY respectfully YOUR STATE Secretary of State; also but not limited to; by any public officer(s) agent(s) contractor(s) assign(s) employee(s) and subsidiaries of your office, regarding the undersigned's "NOTICE and DEMAND" rendered by registered mail with Liber book number and page affixed. (See front page.)

PAGE THREE LEGAL NOTICE AND DEMAND

(6) Which silence of Corporate Office "Secretary of State" ratifies severance(s) of any nexus or relationship to de facto corporate commercial state office(s); Being fraudulent conveyance by operating under "color of authority" upon affiant. Nonetheless, let this be known by undersigned's "**Good Faith (Oxford) Doctrine**" to all men and women. I do not consent to *any* warrantless search(s), or searches that are not compliant with the "Constitution for the United States of America" and/or all of the Amendments of the Honorable "Bill of Rights" whether of my dwelling(s) car(s), landcraft, watercraft, aircraft, me, mine, current location, property,
hotel room(s), apartment(s), business records, business or my machinery, vehicles, equipment, supplies, buildings, grounds, land in my private possession, or control, past present and future now and forevermore so help you God.

(7) By this record let it be now known, I do not at *any* time waive *any* rights or protections, as acknowledged by the aforementioned Constitution and/or Honorable Bill of Rights, nonetheless, demanding you protect these as you swore an oath to do so. I accept your lawfully required "Oath of Office", Bond(s) of any type, insurance policies, and property of any type for my protection and making whole. Furthermore, should you witness *any* (public) officer(s) at this time, or *any* time past present or future, violate *any* of my rights or protections, it is your sworn duty (of oath) to immediately arrest, or have, them arrested; and charge them as you should *any* law breaker, regardless of (superior) officer(s) title, rank, uniform, cloak, badge, position, stature or office. Hence, or you shall be accountable for monetary gain from, but not limited to, your monetary liability, your corporate bond, compensatory costs, punitive procurements and sanctioned by attorney attributions.

(8) NOTE * A true and correct notarized copy of this **Statute Staple Securities Instrument** is safely deposited in "Register of Deeds" Office in YOUR COUNTY , YOUR STATE, **AND** with several entrusted friends accompanying sworn affidavits certifying my policy of presenting this security instrument to each and every (public) officer whom approaches the undersigned violating my unalienable rights; including, but not limited to, my right of liberty and free movement upon *any* common pathway of travel. I have a lawful right to Travel, by whatever means, via land, sea or air, without there being *any* officer, agent, employee, attorney or judge that in *any* manner willfully *causes* adverse affects or damages upon the undersigned by an arrest, detainment, restraint, deprivation; I will be afforded the status and treatment of a foreign Sovereign, a foreign diplomat, by all customs officials; this document or the deposited copy becomes an evidentiary document certified herein, as if now fully reproduced. Further any court action taken from the undersigned is caused by *your act(s)* under color of law with you, your officers and employees. **Take note**; you are now monetarily liable in your personal corporate capacity. First-Middle:[LastName] [Freeman], a sovereign, notwithstanding anything contrary, abides by all laws in accord with the aforementioned "Bill of Rights" and applicable to sovereigns, and wishes no harm to any man. You agree by your non response to uphold my "Right to Travel" or you must rebut my presumption by lawfully documented evidence in law On and For the Record, Under Oath and penalty of Perjury, within the Thirty (30) Days, as aforementioned in this Admiralty Contract. Definitions as they apply to this contract are enclosed in ATTACHMENT "B", and are included as a legal part of this contract.

PAGE FOUR LEGAL NOTICE AND DEMAND

(9) BE WARNED, NOTICED, AND ADVISED that I rely upon, in addition to constitutional limits of the "Constitution for the United States of America" and/or the Honorable "Bill of Rights", upon governmental authority, the rights and protections guaranteed under Uniform Commercial Code(s), Common Equity Law, Laws of Admiralty, and Commercial Liens and Levies Pursuant, But Not Limited To, Title 42 (Civil Rights)

Title 18 U.S.C.A. (Criminal Codes), Title 28 U.S.C.A. (Civil Codes) and additionally YOUR STATE Constitution

Penal Codes, inasmuch as they are in compliance with aforementioned Constitution and/or Bill of Rights.

There can be no violation of any of these laws unless there is a victim consisting of a Natural flesh and blood Man or Woman who has been damaged. When there is no victim there is no crime, or law broken. Unless this is rebutted within the time limit contained herein, and the conditions of the rebuttal are met, you, or any representative in any capacity of any agency, government, corporation, or the like, agree to abide by this contract anytime you interact with me. The undersigned addresses the foregoing being of lawful majority age, clear head, and sound mind henceforth.

(10) Remember, you took a solemn binding oath to protect and defend the original Constitution for the United States of America (1776) adopted circa (1787). Violation(s) of said oath is perjury being a bad-faith doctrine by constructive treason and immoral dishonor infra ¶13, ¶14 & ¶15. I accept said Oath of Office that you have sworn to uphold. I declare that any and all presumptions that I am citizen, subject, resident, participant, legal entity, strawman, fiction, or any such thing, of any and all jurisdictions of the UNITED

STATES OR ANY OF ITS SUBDIVISIONS, AGENCIES, ENTITIES, DEPARTMENTS, SUBSIDIARIES is now and forever rebutted. You may rebut my presumptions by submitting certified copies of lawful documents that have been certified by the YOUR STATE States Attorney, while under oath and on the official record and under penalty of perjury and waiving all immunities from prosecution. You have Thirty (30) days to rebut my statements, as indicated herein, or my statements will stand as true, lawful and legal in all of your courts, and/or hearings.

(11) This legal and timely notice declaration and demand is prima facie evidence of sufficient Notice of Grace. The terms and conditions of this presentment agreement is a quasi-contract under the Uniform Commercial Code; and Fair Debt Collections Act; as contained, but are not limited to, the waiver on your part of *any* and *all* immunities you may claim, should you in *any* way violate the undersigned or allow violation(s) by others. Your corporate commercial act(s) against me or mine and your failures to act on behalf of me or mine are ultra vires, and injurious by willful and gross negligence.

(12) The liability is upon you, and/or your respondeat superior, and upon others (any and all local, state, regional, federal, multijurisdictional, international, and/or, corporate agencies, and/or persons of the foregoing, involved directly or indirectly with you via any nexus) acting with you; and said liability shall be satisfied jointly and/or severally at my discretion. You are sworn to your Oath of Office, and I accept your Oath of Office and your responsibility to uphold the rights of me and mine at all times.

PAGE FIVE LEGAL NOTICE AND DEMAND

BILLING COSTS ASSESSED WITH LEVIES AND LIENS UPON VIOLATIONS SHALL BE:

(13) Unlawful Arrest, Illegal Arrest, or **Restraint,** or **Distraint, Trespassing/Trespass,** Without a Lawfully Correct and Complete 4TH Amendment Warrant: $2,000,000.00 (Two Million) US Dollars, per occurrence, per officer, or agent involved.

Excessive Bail, Fraudulent Bond, Cruel and Unusual Punishment, Violation of Right to Speedy Trial, Freedom of Speech, Conspiracy, Aid and Abetting, Racketeering, and or Abuse of Authority as per Title 18 U.S.C.A., ' 241 and ' 242, or definitions contained herein, encroachment: $2,000,000.00 (Two Million) US Dollars, per occurrence, per officer, or agent involved.

Assault or Assault and Battery without Weapon: $2,000,000.00 (Two Million) US Dollars, per occurrence, per officer, or agent involved.

Assault and Battery with Weapon: $3,000,000.00 (Three Million) US Dollars, per occurrence, per officer, or agent involved.

Unfounded Accusations by officer of the court: $2,000,000.00 (Two Million) US Dollars, per occurrence, per officer or agent involved.

(14) Denial and or **Abuse of Due Process**: $2,000,000.00 (Two Million) US Dollars, per occurrence, per officer, or agent involved.

Obstruction of Justice: $2,000,000.00 (Two Million) US Dollars, per occurrence, per officer or agent involved.

Unlawful Distraint, Interstate Detainer, or False Imprisonment: $5,000,000.00 (Five Million) US Dollars, per day, per occurrence, per officer, or agent involved, plus 18% annual interest.

Reckless Endangerment, Failure to Identify and/or Present Credentials and/or **Failure to Charge within 48 (Forty-Eight) Hours** after being detained: $2,000,000.00 (Two Million) US Dollars per occurrence, per officer, or agent involved.

Counterfeiting Statute Staple Security Instruments: $2,000,000.00 (Two Million) US Dollars per occurrence, per officer, or agent involved.

PAGE SIX LEGAL NOTICE AND DEMAND

(15) Unlawful Detention or Incarceration: $2,000,000.00 (Two Million) US Dollars per day, per occurrence, per officer, or agent involved.

Incarceration for Civil or Criminal Contempt of court without lawful, documented in law, and valid reason: $2,000,000.00 (Two Million) Us Dollars per day, per occurrence, per officer, or agent involved.

Disrespect by a Judge or Officer of the Court: $2,000,000.00 (Two Million) US Dollars per occurrence, per officer, or agent involved.

Threat, Coercion, Deception, or Attempted Deception by any officer of the court: $2,000,000.00 (Two Million) US Dollars per occurrence, per officer, or agent involved.

Unnecessary Restraint: $2,000,000.00 (Two Million) US Dollars, per occurrence, per officer, or agent involved.

Refusal of Lawful Bailment as Provided by The aforementioned Constitution and/or Honorable "Bill of Rights": $2,000,000.00 (Two Million) US Dollars per day of confinement, to be prorated by the hour as per Trafficant vs. Florida, per occurrence, per officer, per agent involved.

Coercing, or attempted coercing of, the Real Natural man to take responsibility for the Corporate Strawman against the Natural Man and Secured Party's Will: $2,000,000.00 Two Million US Dollars per occurrence, per officer or agent involved. **The placing of an unlawful or improper lien levy, impoundments, or garnishment** against any funds, bank accounts, savings, accounts, retirement funds, investment funds, social security funds, intellectual property, or any other property belonging to the Natural Man or Woman, Secured Party by any agency as aforementioned herein: $2,000,000.00 (Two Million) US Dollars per occurrence, and $100,000.00 (One Hundred Thousand) US Dollars per day Penalty until lien(s), levy(s), impoundment(s), and/or garnishment(s) are ended and all funds reimbursed, and all property returned in the same condition as it was when taken, with 18 % Yearly interest and my declared value of property.

Destruction, deprivation, concealment, defacing, alteration, or theft, of property, including buildings, structures, equipment, furniture, fixtures, and supplies belonging to the Natural Man and Secured Party, will incur a penalty of Total New Replacement Costs of property , as indicated by owner and secured party, including but not limited to purchase price and labor costs for locating, purchasing, packaging, shipping, handling, transportation, delivery, set up, assembly, installation, tips and fees, permits, replacement of computer information and data, Computer hardware and software, computer supplies, office equipment and supplies, or any other legitimate fees and costs associated with total replacement of New Items of the same type, like, kind, and/or quality, and quantity as affected items. The list and description of affected property will be provided by the owner and secured party will be accepted as complete, accurate, and uncontestable by the agency, or representative thereof that caused such action. In addition to the aforementioned cost there will be a $200,000.00 (Two Hundred Thousand) US Dollars per day penalty until property is restored in full, beginning on the first day after the incident, as provided by this contract.

PAGE SEVEN LEGAL NOTICE AND DEMAND
CAVEAT

(16) The aforementioned charges are billing costs deriving from, but not limited to, Uniform Commercial Code(s) and Fair Debt Collection Act, and this contract. They shall be assessed against persons, government bodies and corporate entities supra; or *any* combination(s) therein by collectively and individually ignoring my natural and/or civil rights as American by declaration; aforementioned Honorable "Bill of Rights" and/or Constitution, which establishes jurisdiction for you in your normal course of business. All violations against me, the undersigned, will be assessed per occurrence, per officer, representative or agent, of any agency that is involved in any unlawful action against me, each individually.

(17) By your actions, you shall lack recourse for all claims of immunity from *any* forum; by your officers knowing consent and admission of perpetrating known act(s) by your continued enterprise. This **Statute Staple Securities Instrument** protects my Article III court remedies, under, but not limited to, Title 42 U.S.C.A Title 18 U.S.C.A and Title 28 U.S.C.A exhausting all state maritime article I administrative jurisdiction(s), Title 18 U.S.C.§ 242.

IGNORANCE OF THE LAW IS NO EXCUSE!

(18) **I, One** First-Middle:[LastName], [Freeman], am the principal you are the agent! Fail not to adhere to your oath, lest you be called to answer before one God Supreme Court Exclusive Original Jurisdiction, which is the court of first and last resort, not excluding my "Good Faith Oxford Indoctrination" by my conclusive honorable "Bill of Rights".

(19) This Statute Staple Securities Instrument is not set fourth to threaten, delay, hinder, harass or obstruct, but to protect guaranteed Rights and Protections assuring that at no time my Unalienable Rights are *ever* waived or taken from the undersigned against my will by threats, duress, coercion, fraud, or without my express written consent of waiver. None of the statements contained herein intend to threaten or cause any type of physical or other harm to anyone. The statements contained herein are to notice any person, whether real or corporate, of their potential personal civil and criminal liability if and when they violate my Inalienable Rights as protected by the original Constitution of (1776) adopted circa (1787) and/or "Bill of Rights". A bona fide duplicate of this paperwork is safely archived with those who testify under oath that it is my standard policy to ALWAYS present this to *any* (public) or private officer attempting to violate me and my rights; and it is noted on the record that by implication of said presentment (NOTICE) is rendered by way of registered mail to Your State Secretary of State Secretary Name being prima facie evidence of your receipt and acceptance of this presentment in both your personal and individual capacity jointly and severally for each and all governmental political corporate bodies and other individuals who have been, are now being, or hereinafter, are involved in the instant action(s) or any future action(s) and shall only correspond signing under penalty of perjury pursuant, but not limited to Title 28 U.S.C.A. §1746, as now located placed and found in the Register of Deeds Office in YOUR COUNTY, YOUR STATE **supra.**

PAGE EIGHT LEGAL NOTICE AND DEMAND

SUMMATION

(20) Should you move against me in defiance of this presentment there is no immunity from prosecution available to you, or *any* of your fellow (public) officers, who participate in *any* action(s) or *any* officials of government, Judge, Magistrate, District Attorney, Clerk or *any* other person who becomes involved in the instant action(s) or *any* future action(s) by way of aid and abetting. Take due heed and govern yourself accordingly. **Hence, any or all documents rendered upon the undersigned party lacking bona-fide ink signatures or dates per title 18 U.S.C.A. § 513-514 are counterfeit security instrument(s) causing you to be liable in your corporate and individual capacity(s) by fraudulent conveyance now and forevermore; [EMPHASIS ADDED].** If and when you cause any injury and/or damages to the Natural Man or Woman, Secured Party, by violating any of the rights, civil rights, privileges, or any terms herein, you agree to willingly, with no reservation of rights and defenses, at the written request of the Natural Man or Woman, Secured Party, surrender, including, but not limited to, any and all bonds; public, and/or corporate insurance policies; CAFRA funds; as needed to satisfy any and all claims as filed against you by the Natural Man or Woman, Secured Party. This applies to any and all agents, or representatives, severally and individually, of the UNITED STATES or any of the Subdivisions thereof, as described herein.

**NOTICE TO AGENT IS NOTICE TO PRINCIPAL AND
NOTICE TO PRINCIPAL IS NOTICE TO AGENT**

(21) This document cannot be retracted by *any* employee, agent, representative or officer of the court or any individuals excluding the foregoing Named Title Holder on this "Registered Document" for one hundred years from date notarized on this legally binding **Statute Staple Security Instrument** as set fourth by embossed, or other, Notary seal. Attention Agents, Representatives, or Officers, or such as, of the UNITED STATES or its subdivisions including Local, State, Federal, and/or International or Multinational Governments, Corporations, Agencies, and the like: You have Thirty (30) days to rebut any portion, or all of this document or you stand in total agreement, non response is agreement. Partial response is agreement. Rebuttal must be in written form with legal/lawful, verified, certified documentation in law, with copies of said law enclosed. Notice to Agent is Notice to Principal. Ignorance of the law is no excuse.

PAGE NINE LEGAL NOTICE AND DEMAND

(22) Albeit all other corporations not limited to; Telephone Companies, Cable Companies, Utility Companies, Contractors, Builders, Maintenance Personnel, Investors, Journeymen, Inspectors, Law Enforcement Officers, Officers of the Court, Manufacturers, Wholesalers Retailers and all others, including all persons are bound by all paragraphs and terms herein regardless of Nature of Limited Liability Corporation(s) or Affiliations as "DBA's" "AKA's" Incorporations or any Types of Businesses in Commerce as Deeded by this Securities Agreement and Decree.

(23) YOU ARE FINALY NOTICED having been given knowledge of the law and your personal financial liability in event of *any* violations of my rights and/or being. This **Statute Staple Securities Instrument** now in your hand constitutes timely and sufficient warning by good faith notice and grace. Addendums shall follow.

(24) Dated this_____day of_____, in the year of our Lord Two Thousand Eight. The aforementioned artifacts are presented under the **Good Faith Oxford Doctrine** being of Honor. I accept the Oath of Office of all officers of the Court, including but not limited to the clerk of court, all judges and attorneys from all jurisdictions, all law enforcement officers local, state, federal, international and all agents of the UNITED STATES or any subdivisions thereof.

(25) Any Agent, Law enforcement Officer, Employee, Contractor, Representative, or the like of the "UNITED STATES" or any of its subsidiary's or sub corporations, MAY NOT ENTER ANY PROPERTY AT WHICH I AM LOCATED, LEASE, OWN, or CONTROL, AT ANY TIME, FOR ANY REASON, Without my EXPRESS WRITTEN PERMISSION. Violation of this Notice will be considered Criminal Trespass and subject to a $2,000,000.00(Two Million) lawful US Silver dollar penalty plus damages, per violation, per violator.

PAGE TEN LEGAL NOTICE AND DEMAND

(26) Finally, Any and All Lending Institutions, Brokerage Firms, Credit Unions, Depository Institutions and Insurance Agencies, Credit Bureaus and their Officers, Agents and Employees therein now having been given knowledge of the law as per your own personal financial liability in event of any violations upon First-Middle:[LastName]'s Rights and or Being, this **Statute Staple Securities Instrument** constitutes timely and sufficient warning by Good Faith Notice of your liability regardless of your political affirmations. All penalties contained herein will be subject to a penalty increase of one million dollars per day, plus interest, while there is any unpaid balance for the first (30) days after Default of payment. This penalty will increase by 10% per each day until balance is paid in full, plus 18% annual interest, beginning on the Thirty first (31st) day after Default of payment. All penalties in this document are assessed in Lawful Money and are to be paid in One Troy Ounce US Silver Dollars that are .999% pure silver or equivalent Par Value in Legal Tender or Fiat Paper money. Par value will be determined by the value established by a One Troy ounce .999% pure Silver Coin at the US MINT, or by law, whichever is highest value at the time of the incident. Any dispute over the Par Value will be decided by the Secured Party, or his designee. All definitions in Attachment "B" are included as a part of this contract, and will be applied as written herein. Any dispute of any definition will be the decision of the Secured Party.

A UCC-1 Financial Statement (and/or UCC-3 Addendum thereto) shall follow with articles and attachments as set forth thereon. There is no contradiction of terms as written within confines of this title pursuant to the "Constitution for the United States of America" If any contradiction is found, the meaning will be determined by the Secured Party.

PAGE ELEVEN LEGAL NOTICE AND DEMAND

LS:
⚖

Name: <u> First-Middle:[LastName]   Secured   Party   Grantor   </u>.
Country: <u>The   united   States   of   America</u>
⚖

<u>All Property belonging to the Debtor Belongs to the Secured Party as listed on enclosed ATTACHMENT "A".</u>

<u>   Your Legal Land Desciption Here   </u>.

Street: _____ <u>Your   </u>

<u>Address   </u>. ‾

County: <u> Your County, </u>

City: ___<u> Your City </u>

⚖

State of Origin:___<u> Your State </u>

PAGE TWELVE LEGAL NOTICE AND DEMAND

NOTICE YOUR COUNTY REGISTER OF DEEDS CLERKS

(27) Pursuant to Title 18 U.S.C.A. § 2072 in applicable part: "Whoever, being a clerk (or supervisor) or employee of "UNITED STATES" charged with the duty of receiving securities or holding in trust securities on behalf of any person makes a false report shall be fined $5,000 or imprisoned ten years or both." As synonymous with correlating Your State Compiled Laws; Your State and Federal Civil Procedure Laws; Your State Rules of Court; and all other Your State Codes and Uniform Commercial Codes Separate From Title 18 U.S.C.A. § 2076. Also Title 18 U.S.C.A. § 2071 (a) concealment by supervisors secretaries or clerk(s) verifies in part: "Whoever willfully and unlawfully conceals or attempts to do so" (from any individual) "shall be fined or imprisoned three years or both period." Simply Stated: All "Register of Deed Clerks" are liable for non-compliance to the text herein under due process and obstruction of justice as written on pages five and six, ¶14 & ¶15. This Agreement is Valid at 12:00 Noon on the day that it is recorded, unless rebutted as indicated herein, within Thirty (30) calendar days.

(28) SUBSCRIBED AND AFFIRMED: On this_____day

of_____, 2009 AD before me appeared First-Middle:[LastName], known to me, or proved to me on the basis of satisfactory evidence, to be the man whose name is subscribed on this **Statute Staple Securities Instrument**. Witness my hand and official stamp signed sealed delivered by hand, or by Private Registered/Certified mail now and forever more; Drafted by the above secured party grantor with attached property description.

NS: _____
_____   **Signature of Notary Public**

LS: _____

   FIRST WITNESS
NOTARY SEAL

LS: _____

   SECOND WITNESS

LS: _____

   THIRD WITNESS TRUSTEE

Attachments: Attachment A, NOTICE OF OWNERSHIP
      Attachment B, DEFINITIONS
      Attachment C, Your State **UCC-Secured Transaction Registry-** 123456789   **Attachment D,** Act of State, Reaffirmation of Character, State of Your State **APOSTILLE No.** 123456789

LEGAL NOTICE AND DEMAND

ATTACHMENT "A", NOTICE OF OWNERSHIP

ALL PROPERTY BELONGING TO THE DEBTOR BELONGS TO THE SECURED PARTY INCLUDING BUT NOT LIMITED TO THE FOLLOWING: ALL COMPUTERS AND PERSONAL POSSESSIONS IN ON OR AROUND MY LOCATION, CERTIFICATE OF LIVE BIRTH # 111-22-333333 (Your State), **DRIVERS LICENSE #**31313131, Your State **SOCIAL SECURITY NUMBER** 111-22-3333 **AND ALL VALUE ASSOCIATED WITH THIS ACCOUNT, ALL PERSONAL PROPERTY, and CONTENTS OR ANYTHING OF VALUE ON, IN, OR AROUND, PROPERTY LOCATED AT OR NEAR** Your Address, City, State, Near; [YourZipCode]; **Act of State, Reaffirmation of Character, State of** Your State **APOSTILLE No.** 123456789; **NOTICE AND DEMAND, POWER OF ATTORNEY, AND COMMERCIAL SECURITY AGREEMENT #** Commercial security Agreement #, **FILED WITH** Your **COUNTY REGISTER OF DEEDS, REGISTERED PRIVATE BOND/ACCOUNT NUMBERS, ALL BANK ACCOUNTS FOREIGN AND DOMESTIC. PRIVATE REGISTERED BOND/PROMISSORY NOTE or MONEY ORDER NUMBERS, ALL REGISTERED OFFSET AND INDEMNITY BONDS FILED WITH US TREASURY, ACTUAL AND CONSTRUCTIVE NOTICE, HOLD HARMLESS AGREEMENT, AND BILL OF EXCHANGE.**

ATTACHMENT "B", DEFINITIONS

1. **Unlawful Arrest**: Means restricting a man or woman's right to move about freely without the proper use of a lawful 4th amendment warrant signed by a judge of "Competent Jurisdiction" while under oath. This includes unnecessary use of restraint devices, traffic stops, raids, or any other type of interaction, when an officer is presented with and ignores a "Notice and Demand", "Public Servants Questionnaire", "Right to Travel" Documents, or other documents notifying the officer of the Sovereign Lawful Rights of the Natural Man or Woman, Secured Party Created by God, which is not to be confused with the Corporate Fiction "Strawman", which was created by the state. This includes arrest when a Natural Man or Woman, Secured Party is incarcerated for refusing to sign any citation, arrest due to contempt of court when he or she is not violent or a physical threat to the court, arrest by Internal Revenue Service for failure to produce books, records, or other documents, arrest and refusal of Habeas Corpus, Arrest for conspiracy of any kind without lawfully documented affidavits from at least three (3) eye witnesses, signed under oath and penalty of perjury.

2. **Illegal Arrest**: same as above item # 1, "**Unlawful Arrest**".

3. **Unlawful Detention**: Means restraining a Natural Man or Woman, Secured Party's freedom of movement, and/or Right to Travel, against his will for more than sixty (60) seconds without a properly authorized lawful 4th amendment warrant signed by a judge of competent jurisdiction while under oath. This includes routine traffic stops, raids, random identification checks, security checks, only after the officer, Agent, or Representative has been notified by the Natural Man or Woman and Secured Party of his status and after the officer has been given documents to prove said status, along with up to ten (10) minutes for officer to examine said documents.

4. **Unlawful Distraint**: Means seizure or taking of any property that is lawfully owned or in possession of the Natural Man or Woman, Secured Party without proper probable cause, and/or Due Process, and Lawful 4th Amendment Warrant. This includes any seizure by any officer, agent, representative, in any capacity, or relationship with the "UNITED STATES" or any of its agencies, contractors, subdivisions, subsidiaries, or the like.

5. **Lawful 4ᵗʰ Amendment Warrant**: Means a warrant that follows the provisions of the Fourth Amendment to the original "Constitution for the United States of America". This warrant must not deter from the exact procedures as outlined by the Fourth Amendment.

6. **Right to Speedy Trial**: Means trial will commence within 90 days of the date of arrest.

7. **Interstate Detainer**: Means the same as Unlawful Detainer as when involving a Real Man or Woman, and Secured Party and involving more than one agency or state of the corporation, or any representative, agent, or officer who has any agreement with, contract with, or permission to act on behalf of any municipal corporation of the "UNITED STATES", or any subsidiary, or sub- corporation thereof.

8. **Unlawful Restraint**: Means any action by any officer, agent, representative, contractor, associate, officer of the court, or the like, to prevent, coerce, intimidate, hinder, or in any way limit the right of a Natural Man or Woman from any type of freedom of legal/ lawful speech, travel, movement, action, gesture, writing, utterance, or enjoyment of any right or privilege that is commonly enjoyed by any member of the public, or any Sovereign.

9. **Freedom of Speech**: Means the right to speak open and plainly without the fear of reprisal. This includes the right of a Real Man or Woman, Secured Party to speak at hearings and trials, before magistrates, judges, officers of the court, agents, representatives, or the like, of the UNITED STATES. It also means that no attempt to suppress this right will be made by any officer of the court or of the "UNITED STATES" CORPORATION. No Judge or officer of any court or tribunal will threaten contempt of court for free speech by any Real Man or Woman, Secured Party.

10. **US Dollars**: Means the currently recognized medium of exchange as used by the general public at the time of offense, at par value, equal to one ounce silver dollar equivalent per each dollar unit, as represented in a claim. All claims and damages will be paid at par value as indicated. Par Value will be established by written law or the value established by the US MINT for the purchase of an official One Troy Ounce .999% Pure Silver Coin, whichever is higher at the time of the offense.

11. **Obstruction of Justice**: Means any attempt by any officer of the court or representative of any agency that represents the "UNITED STATES", or any of its subdivisions, agencies, contractors, etc., to deprive, hinder, conceal, coerce, threaten, a Natural Man or Woman, Secured Party in an attempt to prevent him or her any and every opportunity to legally/lawfully defend him/herself by attempting to produce and file lawful documents, and or testimony, to Agents, Officers, Judges, Magistrates, the court, clerk of court, representatives, investigators, in order to settle any legal/lawful controversy. This also includes any attempt by a judge or officer of the court from hindering the Natural Man/ Woman, Secured Party from filing, admitting, presenting, discussing, questioning, or using any evidence, document, paper, photographs, audio and/or video recordings, or any other type of evidence that they desire to submit as evidence in any type of court proceeding. The determination of what is evidence and what will be admitted is to be solely determined by the Natural Man or Woman, Secured Party. Any evidence will be tried on merits of the lawful content and validity. Any Judge , or officer of the court who attempts to suppress or dismiss legal or lawful evidence will voluntarily surrender all bonds, insurance, property, corporate property, bank accounts, savings accounts, or any corporate property of value to the Natural Man or Woman, secured party upon written demand and surrender all rights to and defenses against said property. This also includes evidence that is supported by case law. This includes attempts by any officer of the court from making motions, order such as Gag Orders or any other means of keeping information suppressed from the public or the official record. The determination of whether the acts of the court are an attempt to suppress evidence will be solely determined by the Natural Man and Secured Party. This also includes the provision as indicated in item # 18 "**Racketeering**".

12. **Excessive Bail**: Means any amount of Bail set at an unreasonable rate as per the 8th amendment of the Constitution for the United States of America. This also means bail in excess of the amount of the fine, penalty, or Penal Sum that is associated with the alleged crime committed. This also means that if a Natural Man or Woman, Secured Party has lived in a community or has lived in one community or area for more than one year, (provided that they have not recently moved within a year), works a regular job, or is a member of or involved with a church group, civic group, community enterprise, or can produce at least two affidavits from members of his

community or area stating that he is involved with his community, he cannot be held without bail as a flight risk or a threat to society. If the Natural Man or Woman, Secured Party can produce at least Four (4) affidavits stating that he lives, works, and is involved in his community, (or the prior community in which he lived) he must be released on his own recognizance without any bail required. This provision does not apply to anyone charged with rape, murder, "drug"or violent crimes against women or children.

13. **Cruel and Unusual Punishment**: Means physical violence of any type or form that is used against a Natural Man or Woman, Secured Party that causes visible physical injury i.e. marks, scrapes, scratches, bruises, abrasion, avulsions, fractures, sprains, restraint marks, dislocations, punctures, cuts, loss of blood, loss of body fluids, or any other type of physical stress to the body; or any chemically induced altered mental state of the Natural Man or Woman, Secured Party. This also includes any attempt to incarcerate, restrain, question, detain, withholding food when requested, withholding drink when requested, withholding medications as requested, withhold use of bathroom facilities and supplies when requested, withhold reading and writing materials, withholding communication with friends, family, legal counsel, and religious counsel. Withholding proper clothing as needed for comfort, withholding blankets when requested, withholding hot and cold water for showers, withholding freedom when requested. This also includes ridicule, coercion, threats, verbal insults, rude and offensive language, veiled threats, or any other type of mental stress or anguish.

14. **Conspiracy**: Means the cooperation of two or more persons working together to, restrict, suppress, inhibit, or in any way deprive a Natural Man or Woman, Secured Party of any right, benefit, or privilege that would ordinarily be offered by the Constitution for the United States of America, and/or the Bill of Rights, and/or to any member of the general American public, or to a Sovereign. This also includes the provisions in item # 18, "**Racketeering**".

15. **Victim**: Means any Natural Man or Woman, Secured Party who has received direct damages to themselves or their property as the result of an unlawful or illegal act by another.

16. **Victimless Laws**: Means any law that is passed or presumed to be passed that creates a violation of law where no Natural Man or Woman, Secured party has been damaged. This includes any Statute, Ordinance, Regulation, Policy, or Color of Law provision. These types of laws will not be used in any action, of any kind, against any Natural Man or Woman, Secured Party.

17. **Aiding and Abetting**: means the efforts of any officer, agent, or representative of the UNITED STATES or officer of the court, to assist another of the same to hinder, coerce, restrict, resist, suppress, or deprive in any way, a Natural Man or Woman, Secured Party from receiving any and all rights, benefits, privileges, as provided by the Constitution for the United States of America, and/or the Bill of Rights, or that would normally be offered to the general American public, or a Sovereign. This also includes the provisions as provided in item # 18 "**Racketeering**" and suppression of evidence.

18. **Racketeering**: Means any attempt by any two or more officers of the corporation to restrict, suppress, coerce, manipulate, inhibit, or in any way deprive a Natural Man or Woman, Secured Party from receiving every right, benefit, or privilege that is outlined by the Constitution of the United States of America, and/or the Bill of Rights. This also includes any effort by the officers of the court to hinder, in any way the introduction of evidence, law, facts, affidavits, statements, witness testimony, or any information that is considered relevant by the Natural Man or Woman, Secured Party, or any attempt to prevent a jury from hearing this evidence. This also includes any attempt to prevent this evidence from being heard in a public forum, and before any and all members of the general public, as many as can be accommodated by the main courtroom. All hearings, tribunals, or trials will be held in a public place, and any and all members of the general public will be allowed to attend, without restriction. This also includes questioning and/or interrogation by police officers before, during, and after an arrest.

19. **Federal Zone**: Means any land, property, building, area, zone, 911 zone or Postal Zone that is presumed to be within the territorial jurisdiction of the "UNITED STATES", or any of its representatives as defined herein. This does not include any land, property, building, structure, dwelling, area, zone, that is held by deed, title, warranty deed, contract, or any written or verbal agreement, or any such thing, by a

Natural Man or Woman, or Secured Party, which is located outside of "WASHINGTON, D.C." proper. All privately held properties, of any type, that are being held by any Natural Man or Woman are excluded from any federal zone or any jurisdiction of any representatives of the "UNITED STATES" or any of it's territories. This is fact and may be presented in any court by Affidavit of any Natural Man or Woman, Secured Party of interest involved in any interaction of the "UNITED STATES", or any of its representatives, as outlined in this contract.

20. **State**: Means any of the fifty areas known as states of the "united States of America", which is not the same as the "UNITED STATES" corporation. These are designated by UPPER CASE spelling vs. Upper and Lower Cased spelling of the Name of each State. The all UPPER CASED NAME denotes that this STATE is a part of the "UNITED STATES" corporation, whereas the spelling of the Upper and Lower Cased Name denotes that it is not a part of the "UNITED STATES". This will be determined by the Natural Man or Woman, Secured Party as a condition of this contract. The Natural Man or Woman will also determine whether their State is a part of the jurisdiction of the "UNITED STATES", or not, and will never be challenged by any representative of the "UNITED STATES". The Real Man or Woman, Secured Party will determine if the alleged offense occurred within the limits of the "UNITED STATES". A violation of this provision will be Unlawful Determination and punishable as indicated by this contract agreement.

21. **Trespassing/Trespass -** Means the entry into, or onto the domain, property, residence, area, location, grounds, dwellings, buildings, barns, sheds, caves, structures, lands, storage areas, tunnels, automobiles, trucks, safe houses, underground shelters, automobiles, motor vehicles, recreational vehicles, boats, planes, trains, ships, containers, vans, heavy equipment, farm implements, culverts, driveways, trees, yards, real property, real estate, land, etc., of the Natural Man or Woman, Secured Party without his express written permission, or without a lawfully executed Fourth (4th) Amendment warrant, and any and all agents, or representatives, of the Corporation will fully and completely observe any and all protections as Outlined in the Constitution for the United States of America and/or the Bill of Rights. Any personal property that is damaged, lost, stolen, or misplaced, etc. will be recoverable as indicated in this Notice and Demand document. I solemnly swear affirm that I do not have any illegal contraband on my property, I have never had any illegal contraband on or around my property and never will. Any contraband if it is found on my property will be introduced by the officers or agents during time of trespass. I simply do not allow it on my property. Contraband or illegal items if they are found in a search do not belong to me and may not be used in any attempt in any claim against me. Any and all officers, agents, and representatives of the Corporation will be held individually liable for the full amount of damages as outlined in this Notice and Demand document for trespassing.

22. **Natural Man or Woman, Secured Party**: Means any flesh and blood, living, breathing Man or Woman, created by God, who notifies any representative of the Corporation, verbally or in writing, that he is a Sovereign, Non "UNITED STATES " corporate citizen, Freeman or Freewoman, and not subject to the jurisdiction of the corporation or any of its representatives. This is not to be confused with the Fictitious Legal Entity that was created by the state and is represented by an All CAPITAL LETTER NAME. Any attempt to notify any officer, agent, and representative, of the Status of the Real Man or Woman, Secured Party will be sufficient notice. Sufficient Notice will be determined by oath, statement, or affidavit by the Real Man or Woman, Secured Party and the validity of such will not be challenged by any officer of the court.

23. **County or City**: Means any subdivision of any State of the "United States of America". This term excludes any Jurisdiction, zone, or territory of the "UNITED STATES" corporation unless described by the Natural Man or Woman, Secured Party in all CAPITAL letters. Any dispute over any errors contained in spelling or grammar will be resolved at the discretion of the Natural Man or Woman, Secured Party and will not be challenged by any representative of the corporation.

24. **Agency, Entity, Department, Sub Division, Subsidiary, Contractor, Employee, Inspector, Investigator, Organization, Officer, Agent, Authorized Representative, Policeman, Participant**: are all included to mean any person, corporation, or entity of any kind, who works for, is compensated all or in part by, receives funds, or collects funds for, contracts with, receives any benefit from, receives any privilege from, participates with, has allegiance to, or in any way has a relationship with, the "UNITED STATES" or any of its sub corporations, subsidiaries, sub corporations, departments, or Agencies, etc.

25. **Contract**: Any agreement in writing that has been offered for review and acceptance by another party wherein the offering party has ten (10) days or more, or as stipulated in the contract, to review and respond, accept or rebut, any provisions of the contract, as indicated in the contract, Non Response on the part of the receiving party or agent of the receiving party will be a lawful offer and acceptance of all the terms and conditions contained in said contract. Rebuttal, by the receiving party, of any provision, of the contract, by any other means as is indicated in the contract will be non response. Return of the contract unopened and/or without review will be acceptance, of all conditions, of said contract. Filing contract with the clerk of court or any public records officer will be a lawful offer and notification, and will be presentment to all officers of the court in that state or county. Notice to Agent is Notice to the Principal and Notice to the Principal is notice to the Agent.

26. **False Imprisonment**: Means any attempt by any officer of the court or corporation to incarcerate any Natural Man or Woman, Secured Party against their will and/or against any and all protections of the laws, and provisions of the "Constitution for the United States of America" and/or the Honorable "Bill of Rights".

27. **Representative**: Means any agent, agency, department, officer, investigator, entity, subsidiary, sub-corporation, contractor, employee, inspector, Individual or corporation that has any affiliation, association, collects or distributes funds for, does any task for, receives any benefit or privilege from etc., of or for the "UNITED STATES" or anyone, or anything that represents the interests of, or is being funded by, or receives funds from, or has any attachment to, the "UNITED STATES", or any of its sub divisions, or sub-corporations.

28. **Corporation**: Means any representative, agency, sub corporation, contractor, or any person or entity, that is employed by, receives or distributes funds for, receives any benefit or privilege from, or has any relationship of any kind with the "UNITED STATES" corporation.

29. **Interpretation**: Means if any conflict arises concerning the definition of any of the terms and or conditions of this contract, the conflict concerning the meaning of the term or condition, will be decided by the Natural Man or Woman, Secured Party. Their decision will be final and not subject to review or argument. No liability or penalty will be incurred by the Natural Man or Woman, Secured Party, due to their interpretation of such term and or condition.

30. **Corporate Capacity**: Means acting for, or on behalf of, a corporation, or government entity, while under law or color of law.

31. **Legal Counsel**: The choice of a Natural Man or Woman, to have legal assistance from anyone of their choice whether they are or are not Licensed, or Barred attorneys, Lawyers, Barristers, etc. They may assist, represent, speak on behalf of, write cases for, or perform any act in or out of court for the Natural Man or Woman, Secured party without any hindrance, threat, prosecution, charge, repercussion, from any officer of the court, or representative of the "UNITED STATES" corporation, or any representative, officer, or agent thereof.

32. **Abuse of Authority**: Anyone who denies, withholds, refuses, deprives, limits, inhibits, counteracts, conceals, any right, benefit, protections, or privilege, as protected by the "Constitution for the United States of America" and/or the honorable "Bill of Rights". This includes arrest or detainment without documented

evidence that a lawful crime has been committed by the Natural Man or Woman, Secured Party. This includes use of restraint devices on a Natural Man or Woman, Secured Party and/or physical abuse that makes any marks, scars, cuts, abrasions, or the like. This also includes denial of lawful Due Process, habeas corpus, Excessive Bail, unlawful arrest, unlawful detention, or the like, as outlined in this contract.

33. **Verbal Abuse**: Means the use of offensive, and /or threatening verbal words, body language, and non verbal gestures or actions by any representative of the corporation, as defined herein, upon a Natural Man or Woman, Secured Party. If a controversy arises about an incident the version told by the Natural Man or Woman, Secured Party will be accepted as truth and will not be contested.

34. **Assault and Battery with Weapon**: Means any use of, threatened, or perceived use of any weapon, against me or mine, by any representative of the "UNITED STATES" corporation that creates an atmosphere of fear for the Natural Man or Woman, Secured Party. This includes non lethal weapons, such as tazers, stun guns, mace, pepper spray, any chemical used to incapacitate, rubber bullets, shock force weapons, electronic weapon or any other type of weapon that may be used to control, or to create fear. If a conflict arises about the events the version told by the Natural Man or Woman, Secured Party will be accepted as truth and will not be contested.

35. **Unfounded Accusations**: Means any accusation, charge, or claim, civil or criminal, or in admiralty, that is alleged or made by any representative of the "UNITED STATES" corporation, as defined herein, that is not proven by written documented evidence presented under oath and penalty of perjury, by an authorized agent or representative of the corporation. The accuser has Eight (8) hours to provide said documents to be reviewed and in possession of the Natural Man or Woman, Secured Party; and failure to do so will be unfounded accusations and subject to the penalties contained herein.

36. **Encroachment**: To invade, intrude, or in any way prevent another the full and complete use of property, including trespass, impeding ingress or egress to the property of a Natural Man or Woman, Secured Party, to limit the ability of a Natural Man or Woman, Secured Party to freely access, claim, hold, possess, use, convey, sell, rent, lease, barter, exchange, or in any way, make full unfettered use of their property. This includes the application of unlawful liens and encumbrances of any and all property including wages, salaries, stocks, bonds, bank accounts,(foreign or domestic), savings accounts, contents of safety deposit boxes, gold, silver, notes, insurance funds, annuities, retirement accounts, social security benefits, motor vehicles, automobiles, recreational vehicles, land, real estate, homes, structures, roads, driveways, personal property of any kind, that is held by title, deed, contract, agreement (written or verbal), or is in possession of a Natural Man or Woman, Secured Party. This includes, but is not limited to, traffic stops, searches of vehicles, home invasion, confiscation of any lawful property owned by, in possession of, or under the control of the Natural Man or Woman, Secured Party.

37. **Assault and Battery without a Weapon**: Means the verbal abuse or physical contact, of any kind, upon a Natural Man or Woman, Secured Party without their express voluntary written consent. If a conflict arises about the facts involving the incident the version as told by the Natural Man or Woman, Secured Party will be accepted as truth, without question and will not be contested.

38. **Abuse of Due Process**: Means any action against a Natural Man or Woman, Secured Party, that does not abide by all the rights and defenses contained in or represented by the "Constitution for the United States of America" and/or the Honorable "Bill of Rights". This includes any charge, or claim, civil or criminal, or in admiralty, that is alleged or made by any representative of the "UNITED STATES" corporation.

39. **Denial of Due Process**: Means any attempt by any officer of the court and or corporation to deny, deprive, restrict, prevent, or in any way inhibit the proper Due Process to any Natural Man or Woman, Secured Party as outlined in the "Constitution for the United States of America" and/or the Honorable "Bill of Rights" . Any Public Law, Statute, Regulation, Ordinance, Home Rule, etc., that is

incompatible with the aforementioned Constitution and/or Honorable "Bill of Rights" is null and void and will not be used in any action against any Natural Man or Woman, Secured Party.

40. **Unlawful Detainer**: Means any attempt by any officer of the court or representative of the corporation to arrest, check, hinder, delay, possess, hold, keep in custody, restrain, retard, stop, withhold, a Natural Man or Woman without affording them every protection as outlined by the "Constitution for the United States of America" and/or the Honorable "Bill of Rights". Any Public law, statute, regulation, ordinance or the like will be null and void and will not be used in any action in which a Natural Man or Woman, Secured Party is involved.

41. **Reckless Endangerment**: Means any attempt by any officer of the court or corporation, as defined herein, to endanger, attempt, or threaten to attempt to endanger the life or property of any Natural Man or Woman, Secured Party. This includes dangerous driving in a car, use or threatened use of lethal or non lethal weapons, or chemicals, improper use of restraint devices, use of restraint devices on a non combative Natural Man or Woman, Secured Party. If a conflict rises as to whether or not reckless endangerment has occurred the version of the Natural Man and Secured party will be considered as truth.

42. **Failure to Respond**: Means any attempt by any officer or representative of the corporation to ignore, inhibit, withhold, delay, or deny, a request for information from a Natural Man or Woman, Secured Party.

43. **Failure to Charge within Forty Eight (48) Hours**: Means any attempt by any officer or representative of a corporation to delay, inhibit, prevent, or in any way stop a Natural Man or Woman, Secured Party from being lawfully charged by the court within Forty Eight (48) Hours of Arrest.

44. **Failure to Identify**: Means any time a Natural Man or Woman, Secured Party has interaction with any officer or representative of the court or corporation, the officer or representative must, upon request of the Natural Man or Woman, Secured Party, provide proper identification, written proof of authority, state what his business is with the Natural Man or Woman, Secured Party, complete a public servants questionnaire in advance of arrest or detention, provide documentation properly identifying the officer or respondeat superior's name and contact information and any other relevant information as requested by the Natural Man or Woman, Secured Party. The officer may not detain the Natural Man or Woman, Secured Party for more than Ten (10) minutes while he obtains this information.

45. **Counterfeiting Statute Staple Securities Instruments**: Means any attempt by any officer or representative of a corporation to copy, duplicate, replicate, any document that has "Statute Staple Securities Agreement" typed, printed, or hand written anywhere on the document, without the express written voluntary permission of the document's owner who is the Natural Man or Woman, Secured Party who filed said document in the public record, or is in possession of said document, or who is the maker of said document. If a dispute about permission to duplicate arises, the statements of the Natural Man or Woman, Secured Party, will be accepted as fact without question and will not be contested.

46. **Coercion or Attempt to Coerce**: Means any attempt by any officer or representative of a corporation to threaten, intimidate, deprive, conceal, or in any way prevent a Natural Man or Woman, Secured Party from receiving and/or enjoying any right, or privilege that is granted, outlined, or secured by the "Constitution for the United States of America" and/or the Honorable "Bill of Rights", or allow another to do so.

47. **Purchase Price**: Means the new replacement costs of items of property at the time of replacement. This includes locating, packing, shipping, handling, delivery, set up, installation, and any other fee associated with total replacement of property.

48. **Destruction of Property**: Means any alteration, damage, deprivation, defacing, removing, changing, breaking, separating, removing parts from, erasing of files from, throwing, shooting, kicking, stomping, smashing, crushing, or the like (of) any

property belonging to or in possession of the Natural Man or Woman, Secured Party.

49. **Deprivation of Rights or Property**: Means the concealment, keeping from, hiding, obstructing any rights property or privileges that are outlined or protected by the "Constitution for the United States of America" and/or the "Bill of Rights".

50. **Concealment**: Means hiding or keeping information about property and/or rights from a Natural Man or Woman, Secured Party that should normally be revealed. This includes keeping evidence or law from a jury that could favorably alter the outcome of a case to the benefit of the Natural Man or Woman, Secured Party. No officer of any court, or representative of a corporation, may conceal any law and/or any evidence of any kind that is considered relevant by the Natural Man or Woman, Secured Party; and/or fail to disclose any law that benefits the Natural Man or Woman, Secured Party.

51. **Defacing**: Means the changing or altering the appearance of an item. This also includes changing or altering the meaning of laws, rights, property, documents, or any other thing that has value as determined by the Natural Man or Woman, Secured Party.

52. **Constitution**: Means, for the purpose of this contract, "The Constitution for the United States of America" circa 1791, as opposed to the "Constitution of the UNITED STATES" corporation circa 1868.

53. **Bill of Rights**: Means, for the purposes of this contract, the original "Bill of Rights" circa 1791.

54. **Rights and Defenses**: Means one's legal and/or lawful right and/or ability to defend himself/herself in any action. Upon agreement, the defendant in an action may give up his right to defend himself/herself in a given action. This includes tacit agreement or agreement by default; and the Natural Man or Woman, Secured Party, is never the defendant.

55. **Willingly**: Means a Natural Man or Woman, Secured Party is in full knowledge, agreement, and with full consent, at all times, without fear of reprisal or under threat, or coercion, to any interaction that they in which they are involved with any

agent, officer or representative of any court or corporation, including incorporated governments.

56. **Individual Capacity**: Means acting on ones behalf to do a thing. The officer, representative, agent, or the like, may be acting under law or color of law and go outside of the capacity of the law and take on a personal liability.

57. **Natural Man or Woman**: Means a flesh and blood living breathing Natural Man or Woman, as represented by the Upper and Lower Cased Name; includes "Real Man", "Real Man/Woman". This is not to be confused with the Fictitious Legal Entity that was created by the State that is represented by the all Capital Letter Name.

58. **Artificial Person**: Means a fictitious entity that was created by the state for transacting commerce. This artificial Man or Strawman is represented by the all capital letter name that appears to be spelled the same as the name of the Natural Man or Woman. When the Artificial Person is claimed by the Natural Man or Woman, Secured Party, it is a transmitting utility.

59. **Written or Verbal Agreement**: Means any agreement entered into by a Natural Man or Woman, whether written or verbal. Any question of any contract will be resolved by an affidavit from the Natural Man or Woman, Secured Party. Their affidavit will be considered fact in any action or dispute, without question of any officer, agent, or representative of any corporation, including incorporated governments.

60. **Unlawful Determination**: Means any statement, speech, gesture, writing, presentment, or the like that suggests an idea that negatively represents the character, actions, plans, procedures, customs, ways, of a Natural Man or Woman, Secured Party, or group of Natural Men and/or Women, that is not proven by documented authorized certified evidence, on and for the record under penalty of perjury. This includes off color statements, accusations, or remarks by a judge or other officer of the court and any other representative of any corporation including incorporated governments.

61. **Statute Staple Securities Instrument**: A registered (by way of the post office registered mail) bond, statute, which establishes a procedure for settlement of

commercial debt or obligation of record. Establishes the law as it relates to the Sovereign (Natural) Man or Woman.

62. **Clerk of the Public Record**: Means any clerk employed by a county, state, municipality, federal government, international, multi-national, multijurisdictional, or multi-international who records documents, like this document.

63. **Public Record**: Means any record (document) recorded into the public by the Sovereign or designee; for example, when this document is recorded at a Register of Deeds Office, it becomes a public record.

64. **Presumption(s)**: Legal assumption(s) or inference(s) that places the burden of proof or burden of production on the other party, but never on the Sovereign or His; and no Presumption shall prevail against the Sovereign or His without lawful documented evidence to the contrary on and for the record under penalty of perjury.

65. **Unalienable Rights**: Natural Rights given by God as acknowledged by the Law of Nations and incorporated into the "Bill of Rights" such as, but not limited to, Right to Bear Arms, Freedom of Speech, Right to Trial by a Jury of yours Peers, Right to Due Process, Right of Habeas Corpus, Right to be Exempt from Levy as a Sovereign Creditor, Right to Secured in my private papers and effects.

66. **Right to Travel**: The right to freely move about and/or control any type of craft by whatever means, via land, sea or air, without there being any officer, agent, employee, attorney or judge that in any manner willfully causes adverse affects or damages upon the undersigned by an arrest, inhibition, detainment, restraint, deprivation.

67. **Disrespect** - Anything said or written to me, about me or mine that I do not like, including body language, or anything that makes me or any reasonable man uncomfortable, or have fear,

68. **The Placing or Filing of an Unlawful Lien, Levy, Garnishment, or Attachment**: Means any attempt by any officer, agent or representative of a corporation to place a lien, levy, garnishment, or attachment on the property or collateral of a Natural Man or Woman, Secured Party (hereinafter referred to as Secured Party), without first proving the authority to do so by lawfully documented evidence; furnishing all documents, forms and papers as necessary to prove their authority to do so to a neutral Three (3) Notary Panel (hereinafter referred to as The Panel) selected by the Secured Party; guaranteeing in writing, that the officer or representative signing said documents will be personally liable for any damage(s) due to his unlawful and/or illegal actions; supply bonds or other lawful funds to be held in trust by The Panel until it is identified, by The Panel, whether any actions of the officer, agent or representative have violated any laws or caused damage to the Secured Party. The Panel will have the sole power to determine if any damage(s) has occurred and will release the funds according to The Panel's adjudication. The decision of The Panel will be final with no recourse. The surety bonds and/or funds, held in escrow by The Panel, must be at least Four (4) times the estimated value of the property that is liened, levied, garnished, or attached. The assessment of value will be filed via affidavit by the Secured Party, owner/ possessor to The Panel. The Panel's determination and the assessment thereof will be accepted as truth without question or recourse. You agree to surrender, including, but not limited to, any and all surety bonds; public, and/or corporate insurance policies; CAFRA funds; corporate property; as needed to satisfy any and all claims and/or assessments as filed against you by the Secured Party. You agree that any and all property or collateral with a current or existing lien will remain in the custody and control of the Secured Party until such time that a determination has been made by a jury of twelve of the Peers (as defined herein). In the event that a jury of twelve of the Peers cannot be convened or has not been convened within sixty (60) days from the date of the order of the lien, levy, attachment or garnishment, any action not of the Secured Party shall be dismissed with prejudice and every lien, levy, attachment or garnishment shall be released within ten (10) days and all property rights restored, unencumbered or the officer, agent or representative who authorized said lien, levy, attachment or garnishment agrees to surrender, including, but not limited to, any

and all surety bonds; public, and/or corporate insurance policies; CAFRA funds; corporate property; as needed to satisfy any and all claims and/or assessments as filed against you by the Secured Party (¶15).

69. **Peers**: Same definition as **Natural Man or Woman, Secured Party.**

70. **Ignore** - To refuse or in any way to deny a lawful request for an officer to complete legal documents that will provide information when requested by the Natural Man or Woman, Secured Party.

AFFIDAVIT OF TRUTH

Many organizations provide services individuals can apply to change their status from "tax slave" or "feudal subject of the government" to Sovereign Individual. Some organizations provide you with hundreds of pages of documentation you send to dozens of government agencies. They more or less do everything for you. Other organizations provide courses in which they teach you how to do it yourself. They don't want you to become dependent on them. Typically, these services cost anything from $500 to $10,000.

We have developed a simple approach that may achieve the same objective an "Affidavit of Truth" you file with the local County Recorder. You don't send it to any government agencies - so you minimize the risk of raising "red flags" and being put on government "hit lists."

The Affidavit of Truth is a 12-page document that basically states that the person declaring it is a Sovereign Individual or "freeborn Sovereign" consistent with the tradition of natural common law. Several U.S. Supreme Court cases are cited in support of this declaration.

The Affidavit then declares that any supposed "hidden" or "adhesion" contracts, the government might claim have compromised the status of the Sovereign, are null and void from the outset. Specifically covered are:

- The use of Federal Reserve Notes;
- The use of a bank account;
- The use of a Social Security number;
- The use of a driver's license;
- Using state license plates on a car;
- Past tax returns;
- Birth certificate;
- Marriage License;
- Children in public school;
- Declaration of U.S. Citizenship;
- Voter registration;
- Use of 2-letter state abbreviation and zip code.

The Affidavit continues to describe Federal Jurisdiction as defined by the U.S. Constitution and a number of U.S. Supreme Court cases. Then it covers the powers and contractual obligations of government officials and the issue of statutes and regulations contrary to the U.S. Constitution being null and void.

Finally, the Affidavit includes a revocation of any power of attorney the government might claim attaches to the Social Security number and birth certificate.

This Affidavit has not been tested in any court, and we cannot make any claims as to its efficacy.

End of comments.]

RECORDING REQUESTED BY,]

AND WHEN RECORDED RETURN TO:

]

]

NAME

]   STREET/BOX

]

CITY   ]
STATE   (SPACE ABOVE THIS LINE FOR
RECORDER'S
                                USE ONLY)

AFFIDAVIT OF TRUTH

Be it known to all courts, governments, and other parties, that I,

_____,
am a natural, freeborn Sovereign, without subjects. I am neither subject to any entity anywhere, nor
is any entity subject to me. I neither dominate anyone, nor am I dominated.

My authority for this statement is the same as it is for all free Sovereigns everywhere: the age-old, timeless, and universal respect for the intrinsic rights, property, freedoms, and responsibilities of the Sovereign Individual.

I am not a "person" when such term is defined in statutes of the United States or statutes of the several states when such definition includes artificial entities. I refuse to be treated as a federally or state created entity which is only capable of exercising certain rights, privileges, or immunities as specifically granted by federal or state governments.

I voluntarily choose to comply with the man-made laws which serve to bring harmony to society, but no such laws, nor their enforcers, have any authority over me. I am not in any jurisdiction, for I am not of subject status.

Consistent with the eternal tradition of natural common law, unless I have harmed or violated someone or their property, I have committed no crime; and am therefore not subject to any penalty.

I act in accordance with the following U.S. Supreme Court case:

> "The individual may stand upon his constitutional rights as a citizen. He is entitled to carry on his private business in his own way. His power to contract is unlimited. He owes no such duty [to submit his books and papers for an examination] to the State, since he receives nothing therefrom, beyond the protection of his life and property. His rights are such as existed by the law of the land [Common Law] long antecedent to the organization of the State, and can only be taken from him by due process of law, and in accordance with the Constitution. Among his rights are a refusal to incriminate himself, and the immunity of himself and his property from arrest or seizure except under a warrant of the law. He owes nothing to the public so long as he does not trespass upon their rights." Hale v. Henkel, 201 U.S. 43 at 47 (1905).

Thus, be it known to all, that I reserve my natural common law right not to be compelled to perform under any contract that I did not enter into knowingly, voluntarily, and intentionally. And furthermore, I do not accept the liability associated with the compelled and pretended "benefit" of any hidden or unrevealed contract or commercial agreement.

As such, the hidden or unrevealed contracts that supposedly create obligations to perform, for persons of subject status, are inapplicable to me, and are null and void. If I have participated in any of the supposed "benefits" associated with these hidden contracts, I have done so under duress, for lack of any other practical alternative. I may have received such "benefits" but I have not accepted them in a manner that binds me to anything.

Any such participation does not constitute "acceptance" in contract law, because of the absence of full disclosure of any valid "offer," and voluntary consent without misrepresentation or coercion, under contract law. Without a valid voluntary offer and acceptance, knowingly entered into by both parties, there is no "meeting of the minds," and therefore no valid contract. Any supposed "contract" is therefore void, <u>ab initio</u>.

From my age of consent to the date affixed below I have never signed a contract knowingly, willingly, intelligently, and voluntarily whereby I have waived any of my natural common law rights, and, as such, Take Notice that I revoke, cancel, and make void <u>ab initio</u> my signature on any and all contracts, agreements, forms, or any instrument which may be construed in any way to give any agency or department of any federal or state government authority, venue, or jurisdiction over me.

This position is in accordance with the U.S. Supreme Court decision of <u>Brady v. U.S.</u>, 379 U.S. 742 at 748 (1970):

> "Waivers of Constitutional Rights not only must be voluntary, they must be knowingly intelligent acts, done with sufficient awareness of the relevant circumstances and consequences."

Typical examples of such compelled and pretended "benefits" are:

1. The use of Federal Reserve Notes to discharge my debts. I have used these only because in
America, there is no other widely recognized currency.
2. The use of a bank account, with my signature on the bank signature card. If there is any
hidden contract behind the bank signature card, my signature thereon gives no validity to it. The signature is only for verification of identity. I can be obligated to fulfill no hidden or unrevealed contract whatsoever, due to the absence of full

disclosure and voluntary consent.

Likewise, my use of the bank account thereof is due to the absence of a bank not associated with the Federal Reserve system. In general, people have been prevented from issuing their own currencies, and such prevention is in violation of the United States Constitution. Were there an alternative, I would be happy to use it. To not use any bank at all is impossible or very difficult, as everyone knows, in today's marketplace.

3. The use of a Social Security number. The number normally assigned to persons of subject status, I use exceptionally, under duress, only because of the extreme inconvenience of operating without one in today's marketplace, where it is requested by banks, employers, lenders, and many other government agencies and businesses. My reason for using it is <u>not</u> because I wish to participate in the Social Security system, as I don't wish to participate. Let it be known that I use the Social Security number assigned to me for information only.
4. The use of a driver's license. As a free Sovereign, there is no legal requirement for me to have such a license for travelling in my car. Technically, the unrevealed legal purpose of

driver's licenses is commercial in nature. Since I don't carry passengers for hire, there is no law requiring me to have a license to travel for my own pleasure and that of my family and friends. However, because of the lack of education of police officers on this matter, should I be
stopped for any reason and found to be without a license, it is likely I would be ticketed and
fined or obligated to appear in court. Therefore, under duress, I carry a license to avoid extreme inconvenience.

5. State plates on my car. Similarly, even though technically, my car does not fit the legal definition of a "motor vehicle," which is used for commercial purposes, nevertheless, I have
registered it with the state and carry the state plates on it, because to have any other plates or no plates at all, causes me to run the risk of police officer harassment and extreme inconvenience.

6. Past tax returns filed. Any tax returns I may have filed in the past, were filed due to the
dishonest atmosphere of fear and intimidation created by the Internal Revenue Service (IRS)
and the local assessors' offices; not because there is any law requiring me to do so. Once I
discovered that the IRS and other tax agencies have been misinforming the public, I have felt
it is my responsible duty to society to terminate my voluntary participation. Because such returns were filed under Threat, Duress, and Coercion (TDC), and no two-way contract was ever signed with full disclosure, there is nothing in any past filing of returns or payments that
created any valid contract. Therefore, no legal obligation on my part was ever created.

7. Birth Certificate. The fact that a birth certificate was granted to me by a local hospital or government agency when I entered this world, is irrelevant to my Sovereignty. No status, high or low, can be assigned to another person through a piece of paper, without the recipient's full
knowledge and consent. Therefore, such a piece of paper provides date and place information
only. It indicates nothing about jurisdiction, nothing about property ownership, nothing about rights, and nothing about subject status. The only documents that can have any legal meaning, as it concerns my status in society, are those which I have signed as an adult, with full
knowledge and consent, free from misrepresentation or coercion of any kind.

8. Marriage license. The acquisition of a marriage license is now being revealed as being necessary only for slaves. The act of a Sovereign such as myself obtaining such a license, through social custom and ignorance of law, has no legal effect in changing my status. This is
because any such change in status, if any may be supposed to occur, could happen only
through a hidden and unrevealed contract or statute. Since no hidden, unrevealed, and undisclosed information, if it exists, can be lawfully held to be

binding, it is null and void.
9. Children in public school. The attendance of my children in government-supported "public" schools or government-controlled "private" schools does not create any legal tax obligation for
me, nor any other legal obligation, because I never signed a contract agreeing to such obligation for the supposed "privilege" of public school attendance.

If any of my children have attended government supported "public" or controlled "private" schools, such was done under duress and not out of free will. Be it known that I regard "compulsory state education" as a violation of the Thirteenth Amendment to the U.S. Constitution, which states in relevant part:

> "Neither slavery nor involuntary servitude, except as a punishment for crime whereof the party shall have been duly convicted, shall exist within the United States, or any place subject to their jurisdiction."

10. Declaration of Citizenship. Any document I may have ever signed, in which I answered
"yes" to the question, "Are you a U.S. citizen?" - cannot be used to compromise my status as a
Sovereign, nor obligate me to perform in any manner. This is because without full written disclosure of the definition and consequences of such supposed "citizenship," provided in a document bearing my signature given freely without misrepresentation or coercion, there can
be no legally binding contract.

I am not a "United States" citizen subject to its jurisdiction. The United States is an entity created by the U.S. Constitution with jurisdiction as described on the following pages of this Affidavit. I am not a "resident of," an "inhabitant of," a "franchise of," a "subject of," a "ward of," the "property of," the "chattel of," or "subject to the jurisdiction of" any corporate federal government, corporate state government, corporate county government, corporate city government, or corporate municipal body politic created under the authority of the U.S. Constitution. I am not subject to any legislation, department, or agency created by such authorities, nor to the jurisdiction of any employees, officers, or agents deriving their authority therefrom. Further, I am not a subject of the Administrative and Legislative Article IV Courts of the several states, or Article I Courts of the United States, or bound by precedents of such courts, deriving their jurisdiction from said authorities. Take Notice that I hereby revoke, cancel, and make void <u>ab initio</u> any such instrument or any presumed election made by any of the several states or the United States government or any agency or department thereof, that I am or ever have voluntary elected to be treated as a United States citizen subject to its jurisdiction or a resident of any territory, possession, instrumentality or enclave under the sovereignty or exclusive jurisdiction of any of the several states or of the United States as defined in the U.S. Constitution in Article I, Section 8, Clause 17 and Article IV, Section 3, Clause 2.

11. Past voter registration. Similarly, since no obligation to perform in any manner was ever revealed in print, as part of the requirements for the supposed "privilege" to vote for government officials, any such registration on my part cannot be legal evidence of any obligation to perform. Likewise, I have granted NO jurisdiction over me, to any political office. It is my inherent right to vote on elections or issues that I feel affect all of society; NOT because I need anyone to rule over me. On the contrary - I have used the voting process only to instruct my public servants what a Citizen and Sovereign would like done.

12. Use of the 2-letter state code and zip code. My use of the 2-letter state code and zip code in my "address," which is secretly codified to indicate United States "federal zone" jurisdiction, has no effect whatsoever on my Sovereign status. Simply by receiving or sending "mail" through a quasi-federal messenger service, the postal service, at a location indicated with a 2-letter state code and zip code, cannot place me under federal jurisdiction or obligation. Such a presumption would be ludicrous.

I use these codes only for the purposes of information and making it more efficacious for the U.S. Postal Service to deliver my mail.

13. Use of semantics. There are some immature people with mental imbalances, such as the craving to dominate other people, who masquerade as "government." Just because they alter definitions of words in the law books to their supposed advantage, doesn't mean I accept those definitions. The fact that they define the words "person," "address," "mail," "resident," "motor vehicle," "driving," "passenger," "employee," "income," and many others, in ways different from the

common usage, so as to be associated with a subject or slave status, means nothing in real life.

Because the courts have become entangled in the game of semantics, be it known to all courts and all parties, that if I have ever signed any document or spoken any words on record, using words defined by twists in the law books different from the common usage, there can be no effect whatsoever on my Sovereign status in society thereby, nor can there be created any obligation to perform in any manner, by the mere use of such words. Where the meaning in the common dictionary differs from the meaning in the law dictionary, it is the meaning in common dictionary that prevails, because it is more trustworthy.

Such compelled and supposed "benefits" include, but are not limited to, the aforementioned typical examples. My use of such alleged "benefits" is under duress only, and is with full reservation of all my common law rights. I have waived none of my intrinsic rights and freedoms by my use thereof. Furthermore, my use of such compelled "benefits" may be temporary, until better alternatives become available, practical, and widely recognized.

FEDERAL JURISDICTION

It is further relevant to this Affidavit that any violation of my Rights, Freedom, or Property by the U.S. federal government, or any agent thereof, would be an illegal and unlawful excess, clearly outside the limited boundaries of federal jurisdiction. My understanding is that the jurisdiction of the U.S. federal government is defined by Article I, Section 8, Clause 17 of the U.S. Constitution, quoted as follows:

> "The Congress shall have the power . . . To exercise <u>exclusive legislation</u> in <u>all cases</u> whatsoever, <u>over such district (NOT EXCEEDING TEN MILES SQUARE)</u> as may, by cession of particular states and the acceptance of Congress, become <u>the seat of the</u> <u>Government of the United States,</u> [District of Columbia] and to exercise like authority over all places purchased by the consent of the legislature of the state in which the same shall be, for the Erection of Forts, Magazines, Arsenals, dock yards and other needful Buildings; And - To make all laws which shall be necessary and proper for carrying into Execution the foregoing Powers..." [emphasis added]

and Article IV, Section 3, Clause 2:

> "The Congress shall have the Power to dispose of and make all needful Rules and Regulations respecting the Territory or other Property belonging to the United States; and nothing in this Constitution shall be so construed as to Prejudice any Claims of the United States, or of any particular State."

The definition of the "United States" being used here, then, is limited to its territories:

1) The District of Columbia
2) Commonwealth of Puerto Rico
3) U.S. Virgin Islands
4) Guam
5) American Samoa
6) Northern Mariana Islands
7) Trust Territory of the Pacific Islands
8) Military bases within the several states
9) Federal agencies within the several states

It does not include the several states themselves, as is confirmed by the following cites:

> "We have in our political system a Government of the United States and a government of each of the several States. Each one of these governments is distinct from the others, and each has citizens of its own who owe it allegiance, and whose rights, within its jurisdiction, it must protect. The same person may be at the same time a citizen of the United States and a Citizen of a State, but his rights of citizenship under one of these governments will be different from those he has under the other." Slaughter House Cases <u>United States vs. Cruikshank</u>, 92 U.S. 542 (1875).

"THE UNITED STATES GOVERNMENT IS A FOREIGN
CORPORATION WITH RESPECT TO A STATE." [emphasis added]
<u>Volume 20: Corpus Juris Sec</u>. §1785: NY re: Merriam 36 N.E. 505 1441
S.Ct.1973, 41 L.Ed.287.

This is further confirmed by the following quote from the Internal Revenue Service:

Federal jurisdiction "includes the District of Columbia, the Commonwealth of Puerto
Rico, the Virgin Islands, Guam, and American Samoa." - Internal Revenue Code Section
312(e).

In legal terminology, the word "includes" means "is limited to."

When referring to this "District" United States, the Internal Revenue Code uses the term "<u>WITHIN</u>" the United States. When referring to the several States, the Internal Revenue Code uses the term "<u>WITHOUT</u>" the United States.

Dozens, perhaps hundreds, of court cases prove that federal jurisdiction is limited to the few federal territory areas above indicated. For example, in two Supreme Court cases, it was decided:

> "The laws of Congress in respect to those matters do not extend into the territorial limits of the states, but have force only in the District of Columbia, and other places that are within the exclusive jurisdiction of the national government," <u>Caha v. United States</u>, 152 U.S., at 215.

> "We think a proper examination of this subject will show that the United States never held any municipal sovereignty, jurisdiction, or right of soil in and to the territory, of which Alabama or any of the new States were formed..."

> "[B]ecause, the United States have no constitutional capacity to exercise municipal jurisdiction, sovereignty, or eminent domain, within the limits of a State or elsewhere, except in the cases in which it is expressly granted..."

> "Alabama is therefore entitled to the sovereignty and jurisdiction over all the territory within her limits, subject to the common law," <u>Pollard v. Hagan</u>, 44 U.S. 221, 223, 228, 229.

Likewise, Title 18 of the United States Code at §7 specifies that the "territorial jurisdiction" of the
United States extends only <u>outside</u> the boundaries of lands belonging to any of the several States.

Therefore, in addition to the fact that no unrevealed federal contract can obligate me to perform in any manner without my fully informed and uncoerced consent, likewise, no federal statutes or regulations apply to me or have any jurisdiction over me. I hereby affirm that I do not reside or work in any federal territory of the "District" United States, and that therefore no U.S. federal government statutes or regulations have any authority over me.

POWERS AND CONTRACTUAL OBLIGATIONS OF UNITED STATES AND STATE GOVERNMENT OFFICIALS

All United States and State government officials are hereby put on notice that I expect them to have recorded valid Oaths of Office in accordance with the U.S. Constitution, Article VI:

> "The Senators and Representatives before mentioned, and the members of the several State Legislatures, and all executive and judicial officers, both of the United States and of the several States, shall be bound by oath or affirmation to support this Constitution..."

I understand that by their Oaths of Office all U.S. and State government officials are contractually bound by the U.S. Constitution as formulated by its framers, and not as "interpreted," subverted, or corrupted by the U.S. Supreme Court or other courts According to the Ninth Amendment to the U.S. Constitution:

> "The enumeration in the Constitution of certain rights shall not be construed to deny or disparage others retained by the people."

and the Tenth Amendment to the U.S. Constitution:

> "The powers not delegated to the United States by the Constitution, nor prohibited by it to the States, are reserved to the States respectively, or to the people."

Thus, my understanding from these Amendments is that the powers of all U.S. and State government officials are limited to those specifically granted by the U.S. Constitution.

I further understand that any laws, statutes, ordinances, regulations, rules, and procedures contrary to the U.S. Constitution, as written by its framers, are null and void, as expressed in the Sixteenth American Jurisprudence Second Edition, Section 177:

> "The general misconception is that any statute passed by legislators bearing the appearance of law constitutes the law of the land. <u>The U.S. Constitution is the supreme law of the land</u>, and any statute, to be valid, must be in agreement. It is impossible for both the Constitution and a law violating it to be valid; one must prevail. This is succinctly stated as follows:
>
> 'The general rule is that an unconstitutional statute, though having the form and name of law, is in reality no law, but is wholly void, and ineffective for any purpose; since unconstitutionality dates from the time of its enactment, and not merely from the date of the decision so branding it. <u>An unconstitutional law, in legal contemplation, is as inoperative as if it had never been passed</u>. Such a statute leaves the question that it purports to settle just as it would be had the statute not been enacted.'
>
> 'Since an unconstitutional law is void, the general principles follow that <u>it imposes no duties, confers no right, creates no office, bestows no power or authority on anyone, affords no protection, and justifies no acts performed under it</u>...'

'A void act cannot be legally consistent with a valid one. An unconstitutional law cannot operate to supersede any existing valid law. Indeed, insofar as a statute runs counter to the fundamental law of the land, it is superseded thereby.'

'<u>No one is bound to obey an unconstitutional law</u> and no courts are bound to enforce it.'" [emphasis added]

and as expressed once again in the U.S. Constitution, Article VI:

"This Constitution, and the laws of the United States which shall be made in pursuance thereof; and all treaties made, or which shall be made, under the authority of the United States, shall be the supreme law of the land; and the judges in every State shall be bound thereby, anything in the Constitution or laws of any State to the contrary notwithstanding."

All U.S. and State government officials are therefore hereby put on notice that any violations of their contractual obligations to act in accordance with their U.S. Constitution, may result in prosecution to the full extent of the law, as well as the application of all available legal remedies to recover
damages suffered by any parties damaged by any actions of U.S. and State government officials in
violation of the U.S. Constitution.

REVOCATION OF POWER OF ATTORNEY

Furthermore, I hereby revoke, rescind, and make void <u>ab initio</u>, all powers of attorney, in fact or otherwise, implied in law or otherwise, signed either by me or anyone else, as it pertains to the Social Security number assigned to me, ___as it pertains to my birth certificate, marriage or business license, or any other licenses or certificates issued by any and all government or quasi-governmental entities, due to the use of various elements of fraud by said agencies to attempt to deprive me of my Sovereignty and/or property.

I hereby waive, cancel, repudiate, and refuse to knowingly accept any alleged "benefit" or gratuity associated with any of the aforementioned licenses, numbers, or certificates. I do hereby revoke and rescind all powers of attorney, in fact or otherwise, signed by me or otherwise, implied in law or otherwise, with or without my consent or knowledge, as it pertains to any and all property, real or personal, corporeal or incorporeal, obtained in the past, present, or future. I am the sole and absolute legal owner and possess allodial title to any and all such property.

Take Notice that I also revoke, cancel, and make void <u>ab initio</u> all powers of attorney, in fact, in presumption, or otherwise, signed either by me or anyone else, claiming to act on my behalf, with or without my consent, as such power of attorney pertains to me or any property owned by me, by, but not limited to, any and all quasi/colorable, public, governmental entities or corporations on the grounds of constructive fraud, concealment, and nondisclosure of pertinent facts.

I affirm that all of the foregoing is true and correct. I affirm that I am of lawful age and am competent to make this Affidavit. I hereby affix my own signature to all of the affirmations in this entire document with explicit reservation of all my unalienable rights and my specific common law right not to be bound by any contract or obligation which I have not entered into knowingly, willingly, voluntarily, and without misrepresentation, duress, or coercion.

The use of notary below is for identification only, and such use does NOT grant any jurisdiction to anyone.

FURTHER AFFIANT SAITH NOT.

Subscribed and sworn, without prejudice, and with all rights reserved, (PRINT NAME BELOW)

_____,
Principal, by Special Appearance, in Propria Persona, proceeding Sui Juris.

       My Hand and Mark as Subscriber   (SIGN NAME
                                                              BELOW)

Date:_____Common Law Seal:_____

On this ____day of_____, 19___, before me, the undersigned, a Notary Public in

and for
_____(state), personally appeared the above-signed, known to me to be the
one whose name is signed on this instrument, and has acknowledged to me that s/he has executed the same.

Signed:_____

Printed Name:_____Date:_____ **My Commission Expires:**_____

color of law

The appearance of a legal right.

The act of a state officer, regardless of whether or not the act is within the limits of his or her authority, is considered an act under color of law if the officer purports to be conducting himself or herself in the course of official duties.

Color of Law Abuses

U.S. law enforcement officers and other officials like judges, prosecutors, and security guards have been given tremendous power by local, state, and federal government agencies—authority they must have to enforce the law and ensure justice in our country. These powers include the authority to detain and arrest suspects, to search and seize property, to bring criminal charges, to make rulings in court, and to use deadly force in certain situations.

Preventing abuse of this authority, however, is equally necessary to the health of our nation's democracy. That's why it's a federal crime for anyone acting under "color of law" willfully to deprive or conspire to deprive a person of a right protected by the Constitution or U.S. law. "Color of law" simply means that the person is using authority given to him or her by a local, state, or federal government agency.

The FBI is the lead federal agency for investigating color of law abuses, which include acts carried out by government officials operating both within and beyond the limits of their lawful authority. Off-duty conduct may be covered if the perpetrator asserted his or her official status in some way.

During 2012, 42 percent of the FBI's total civil rights caseload involved color of law issues—there were 380 color of law cases opened during the year. Most of the cases involved crimes that fell into into five broad areas:

- Excessive force;
- Sexual assaults;
- False arrest and fabrication of evidence;
- Deprivation of property; and
- Failure to keep from harm.

Excessive force: In making arrests, maintaining order, and defending life, law enforcement officers are allowed to use whatever force is "reasonably" necessary. The breadth and scope of the use of force is vast—from just the physical presence of the officer…to the use of deadly force. Violations of federal law occur when it can be shown that the force used was willfully "unreasonable" or "excessive."

Sexual assaults by officials acting under color of law can happen in jails, during traffic stops, or in other settings where officials might use their position of authority to coerce an individual into sexual compliance. The compliance is generally gained because of a threat of an official action against the person if he or she doesn't comply.

False arrest and fabrication of evidence: The Fourth Amendment of the U.S. Constitution guarantees the right against unreasonable searches or seizures. A law enforcement official using authority provided under the color of law is allowed to stop individuals and, under certain circumstances, to search them and retain their property. It is in the abuse of that discretionary power—such as an unlawful detention or illegal confiscation of property—that a violation of a person's civil rights may occur.

Fabricating evidence against or falsely arresting an individual also violates the color of law statute, taking away the person's rights of due process and unreasonable seizure. In the case of deprivation of property, the color of law statute would be violated by unlawfully obtaining or maintaining a person's property, which oversteps or misapplies the official's authority.

The Fourteenth Amendment secures the right to due process; the Eighth Amendment prohibits the use of cruel and unusual punishment. During an arrest or detention, these rights can be violated by the use of force amounting to punishment (summary judgment). The person accused of a crime must be allowed the opportunity to have a trial and should not be subjected to punishment without having been afforded the opportunity of the legal process.

Failure to keep from harm: The public counts on its law enforcement officials to protect local communities. If it's shown that an official willfully failed to keep an individual from harm, that official could be in violation of the color of law statute.

Filing a Complaint

To file a color of law complaint, contact your local FBI office by telephone, in writing, or in person. The following information should be provided:

- All identifying information for the victim(s);
- As much identifying information as possible for the subject(s), including position, rank, and agency employed;
- Date and time of incident;
- Location of incident;
- Names, addresses, and telephone numbers of any witness(es);
- A complete chronology of events; and
- Any report numbers and charges with respect to the incident.

You may also contact the United States Attorney's Office in your district or send a written complaint to:
Assistant Attorney General
Civil Rights Division
Criminal Section
950 Pennsylvania Avenue, Northwest
Washington, DC 20530

FBI investigations vary in length. Once our investigation is complete, we forward the findings to the U.S. Attorney's Office within the local jurisdiction and to the U.S. Department of Justice in Washington, D.C., which decide whether or not to proceed toward prosecution and handle any prosecutions that follow.

Civil Applications
Title 42, U.S.C., Section 14141 makes it unlawful for state or local law enforcement agencies to allow officers to engage in a pattern or practice of conduct that deprives persons of rights protected by the Constitution or U.S. laws. This law, commonly referred to as the Police Misconduct Statute, gives the Department of Justice authority to seek civil remedies in cases where law enforcement agencies have policies or practices that foster a pattern of misconduct by employees. This action is directed against an agency, not against individual officers. The types of issues which may initiate a pattern and practice investigation include:
- Lack of supervision/monitoring of officers' actions;
- Lack of justification or reporting by officers on incidents involving the use of force;
- Lack of, or improper training of, officers; and
- Citizen complaint processes that treat complainants as adversaries.

Under Title 42, U.S.C., Section 1997, the Department of Justice has the ability to initiate civil actions against mental hospitals, retardation facilities, jails, prisons, nursing homes, and juvenile detention facilities when there are allegations of systemic derivations of the constitutional rights of institutionalized persons.

The next page is the first thing I would show the law enforcement officer. If they still won't leave you alone show them you really know the real law with the rest of this book. Most of them don't even know these laws that is how dumb they make these guys so they will do what they want them to and it is not even a law that they are enforcing. What they call laws our just codes.

"I hereby invoke and refuse to waive all of the following rights and privileges afforded to me by the U.S. Constitution:

-I invoke and refuse to waive my Fifth Amendment right to remain silent. DO NOT ASK ME ANY QUESTIONS.

-I invoke and refuse to waive my Sixth Amendment right to an attorney of my choice. DO NOT ASK ME ANY QUESTIONS WITHOUT MY ATTORNEY PRESENT.

-I invoke and refuse to waive all privileges and right pursuant to the case Miranda v. Arizona. DO NOT ASK ME ANY QUESTIONS OR MAKE ANY COMMENT TO ME ABOUT THIS DECISION.

-I invoke and refuse to waive my Fourth Amendment right to be free from unreasonable searches and seizures. I DO NOT CONSENT TO ANY SEARCH OR SEIZURE OF MYSELF, MY HOME, OR OF ANY PROPERTY IN MY POSSESSION. Do not ask me about my ownership interest in any property. I DO NOT CONSENT TO THIS CONTACT WITH YOU. If I am not presently under arrest or under investigatory detention, please ALLOW ME TO LEAVE.

-Any statement I make, or alleged consent I give, in response to your questions is hereby UNDER PROTEST AND UNDER DURESS and in submission to your claim of lawful authority to force me to provide you with the information.

-If you have no Probable cause or RAS and you continue to hold me against my will, you have now opened the door for a Chapter 42 US Code 1983 Civil Rights Law Suit.

am I free to go"?

www.ingramcontent.com/pod-product-compliance
Lightning Source LLC
LaVergne TN
LVHW021158140825
818589LV00043B/927